D1533737

LYNDON BAINES JOHNSON

OUR THIRTY-SIXTH PRESIDENT

by Melissa Maupin

THE CHILD'S WORLD ®

Published in the United States of America

The Child's World®
1980 Lookout Drive • Mankato, MN 56003-1705
800-599-READ • www.childsworld.com

Acknowledgments
The Child's World®: Mary Berendes, Publishing Director

Creative Spark: Mary McGavic, Project Director; Melissa McDaniel, Editorial
Director; Deborah Goodsite, Photo Research

The Design Lab: Kathleen Petelinsek, Design; Gregory Lindholm, Page Production

Content Adviser: David R. Smith, Adjunct Assistant Professor of History,
University of Michigan–Ann Arbor

Photos
Cover and page 3: White House Historical Association (White House Collection)
(detail); White House Historical Association (White House Collection)

Interior: Associated Press Images: 28, 31, 36; Corbis: 12, 14, 17, 33, 34, 37
(Bettmann); Getty Images: 8, 19, 20 and 38, 21, 23 and 39 (Time & Life Pictures),
13 (Myron Davis/Time Life Pictures); iStockphoto: 44 (Tim Fan); Lyndon Baines
Johnson Library: 4, 5, 7, 9 and 38, 10, 15, 18 (unknown), 11 (Underwood &
Underwood, Washington), 25 (Cecil Stoughton), 26 and 39 (Yoichi Okamoto), 29,
30 (Frank Wolfe); SuperStock: 22 (SuperStock, Inc.); U.S. Air Force photo: 45.

Library of Congress Cataloging-in-Publication Data
Maupin, Melissa, 1958–
  Lyndon Baines Johnson / by Melissa Maupin.
    p. cm. — (Presidents of the U.S.A.)
  Includes bibliographical references and index.
  ISBN 978-1-60253-064-5 (library bound : alk. paper)
  1. Johnson, Lyndon B. (Lyndon Baines), 1908–1973—Juvenile literature.
  2. Presidents—United States—Biography—Juvenile literature. I. Title. II. Series.

E847.M375 2008
973.923092—dc22
  [B]
                              2008000615

Lyndon Johnson
served as president
from 1963 to 1969.

TABLE OF CONTENTS

FARM BOY TO POLITICIAN

Like many Texans in the early 1900s, Lyndon Baines Johnson was born and grew up on a farm. His parents, Samuel Johnson and Rebekah Baines Johnson, owned a small farm outside of Stonewall, Texas, in an area called the Hill Country. This part of Texas is filled with rolling hills but is difficult to farm. It is rocky country that often suffers from lack of rainfall. Johnson's family struggled his entire childhood to make a living on the land.

Lyndon Johnson was born on August 27, 1908. A few years later the family moved to Johnson City, 15 miles (24 km) away from Stonewall. Lyndon was the Johnsons' first child, and his parents, particularly his mother, gave him a great deal of attention. Over the

Lyndon Johnson was born and raised in central Texas.

next years, Lyndon would have to share that attention with three sisters—Rebekah, Lucia, and Josefa—and a little brother named Sam.

Lyndon's father had worked as a barber and a teacher besides trying his hand at farming. But he really longed to work in **politics.** In 1904, he was elected to the state **legislature.** Samuel Johnson was respected and intelligent, but he could never make the farm a success, and the family lost money. Lyndon's mother was the daughter of a lawyer. She had gone to college. At the time, this was rare for women. She was often frustrated by the lack of money and security she had in her adult life. Rebekah Johnson wanted a better life

In this photograph from 1910, members of the Johnson family pose in front of their house in Stonewall, Texas.

Lyndon Johnson's parents couldn't agree on his name for the first three weeks of his life. They simply called him "baby." His father finally suggested "Linden" after his friend, a lawyer named W. C. Linden. Rebekah agreed but changed the spelling to "Lyndon" and added her maiden name, "Baines."

Lyndon Johnson was his parents' favorite child. As a boy he often ran away (but only short distances) to draw attention to himself. The family finally installed a bell on the back porch so his mother could alert men working in the fields to help her find him.

for Lyndon. She pushed him to study hard in school, hoping he would make a good living one day.

Lyndon was a bright child but not a great student. He excelled in English and history but barely scraped by in math and science. In high school, he was a prankster who stayed out late at night and sometimes cut classes. Lyndon always preferred the company of adults and older children. His friends were often five to ten years older than he was.

Lyndon graduated from high school when he was 15 years old. One night, he and his friends went out in his father's car and drank some beer. They ended up crashing the car, and Lyndon knew his dad would be furious. To escape punishment, Lyndon fled to a cousin's house near Corpus Christi, a town on the Texas coast. He got a job cleaning cotton but found the work too difficult. He longed to return home.

After his father promised he would not punish him, Lyndon went home. His mother urged him to enroll at Southwest Texas State Teachers College, the college closest to their home. But Lyndon was young and restless. He yearned to see the rest of the country. Lyndon and several of his friends decided to take a road trip to California. Each boy pitched in five dollars to buy an old Model T car. They worked all along the trip doing odd jobs. Once the boys arrived in California, Lyndon took several jobs, including working as an errand boy for a relative in a law firm.

When Lyndon returned to Texas, he got a job building a highway. He earned two dollars a day. He

Samuel Johnson was elected to the Texas House of Representatives six times.

finally signed up for college as his mother wished. As he attended classes, Lyndon also worked at the college to pay for his education. He started out as a janitor but set his sights on better jobs. He used his early political skills to charm the staff. Soon he was the assistant to the secretary of the college president.

Lyndon left school for a year to teach students at Welhausen Ward Elementary School in Cotulla, Texas, near the Mexican border. His students were poor Mexican and Mexican American children. At the time, schools in Texas and elsewhere around the country practiced **segregation.** White students attended different schools than black and Hispanic students. Welhausen, like most schools that served Hispanic

Johnson City, where President Johnson lived as a boy, was named after James Johnson, the town's founder. James was Lyndon's relative.

7

Lyndon's mother had a strong influence on him. She urged him to do well in school and always stand up for his beliefs.

Lyndon Baines Johnson was often simply called "LBJ."

children, had little money to spend on its students. It could offer only a basic education. The school did not have sports teams or other activities. Lyndon saw how unfair this was. He felt moved to improve the lives and education of his students. He held **debates** and set up spelling bees in his classroom. He found money to buy sporting equipment. He hosted baseball games and track meets for the students.

At this early stage in his career, Lyndon Johnson decided that everyone had the right to a better life if they were willing to work for it. Later, as president, he told Americans about a plan to help the nation, which he called the Great Society. He described the Great

Society as "a place where the meaning of a man's life matches the marvels of a man's labor."

After working as a teacher for a year, Lyndon returned to college. He soon found he was more successful with the adults on campus than with the students. Most of the popular students at Southwest Texas College belonged to a group called the Black Stars. But the Black Stars didn't want anything to do with Lyndon. He was considered odd looking. He was tall, skinny, and had big ears. Unlike many of the popular boys in the Black Stars, Lyndon was not an athlete. Lyndon fought back by forming a group called

Lyndon Johnson (back row center) taught fifth, sixth, and seventh grades at Wellhausen Ward Elementary School in Cotulla, Texas. He also coached the boy's baseball team and the debate team. He is shown here with some of his students.

Lyndon's mother convinced him to attend college, but he had to find a way to pay for it. He borrowed $75 and accepted work as a janitor and as an office helper.

the White Stars. It included many students who were outcasts on campus. The White Stars grew in number and power. Soon the White Stars were more powerful on campus than the Black Stars.

Lyndon was an average student in college. He enjoyed writing for the campus paper, the *Star.* As a member of the debate team, he was also a skilled speaker. Just before Lyndon's graduation, a young politician named Welly K. Hopkins heard him give a speech.

Hopkins liked the speech so much that he asked Lyndon to help with his **campaign** for state senate. The young man eagerly made flyers and posters for Hopkins. He asked the White Stars to help him. Hopkins won the election and gave Lyndon much of the credit.

After graduation, Lyndon took a job teaching at Sam Houston High School. One day, he received a call from Richard Kleberg, a U.S. congressman from Texas. Kleberg had talked to Hopkins and heard what a great job Lyndon had done on his campaign. Kleberg asked Lyndon to be his secretary. Lyndon eagerly accepted, and at age 23, he made his first trip to Washington, D.C.

Richard Kleberg was elected to the U.S. House of Representatives in 1931. That same year, Lyndon Johnson became his secretary.

11

A TEXAS LEGACY

Lyndon Johnson was a colorful man. He stood six feet three inches (191 cm) tall, had big ears, and often wore cowboy boots. His looks, his Texas drawl, and his strong personality made him hard to forget. But Johnson never left anything to chance. To make sure future generations remembered him, Johnson helped establish the Lyndon Baines Johnson School of Public Affairs, the Lyndon Baines Johnson Library and Museum, and the Lyndon Baines Johnson National Historical Park.

The LBJ School of Public Affairs is located at the University of Texas in Austin. It is for students who are planning a life in public service. Johnson wanted politicians to teach the students instead of professors. The LBJ Library and Museum, also at the University of Texas, is one of the nation's many presidential libraries. Its eight stories house 44 million documents from Johnson's career. Johnson said of the library, "I hope that visitors who come here will achieve a closer understanding of the presidency and that the young people who come here will get a clearer comprehension of what this nation tried to do in an eventful period of its history."

Shortly after Johnson retired, he and his wife donated a portion of the LBJ Ranch to the National Park Service. Johnson had turned his land into a successful working ranch with 400 head of cattle. He asked the park service to keep his ranch working. Today the ranch, the Johnsons' home, the family cemetery, and a one-room schoolhouse where Johnson went to school are part of one section of the Lyndon Baines Johnson National Historical Park. Another section of the park is 14 miles (23 km) away in Johnson City. It includes the Johnson settlement, his boyhood home, and a visitor center.

CHAPTER TWO

LIFE IN WASHINGTON

Lyndon Johnson came to Washington, D.C., eager to show what he could do. Congressman Kleberg was happy to hand over many duties to his new assistant. Soon, Johnson was practically running Kleberg's office. During this time, he began to meet

Lyndon Johnson moved to Washington, D.C., in 1931. He soon became known for his energy and talent.

Johnson loved politics.
"I seldom think of
politics more than
18 hours a day,"
he once joked.

important leaders and build a career in politics. A natural leader and organizer, Johnson gathered other assistants together to form the "Little Congress." Although his position as a congressman's secretary was not meant to be powerful, he soon became a name to contact in the government when people wanted something done.

During this period of his life, Johnson's personal life also changed. He had never been popular in college with girls and had gone on only a few dates. But then, on a trip through Austin, Texas, Lyndon met Claudia Alta Taylor. He boldly asked her to lunch and she accepted. Claudia was nicknamed "Lady Bird" because her nanny once said she was as pretty as a ladybird (another name for a ladybug). She was from one of the wealthiest families in eastern Texas. Lady Bird was shy and intelligent. She had graduated from the University of Texas where, like Lyndon, she had worked on the campus newspaper. Lyndon Johnson fell in love with her at first sight and proposed to her on their first date. Lady Bird later said she was totally surprised at his proposal. "I thought it was some kind of a joke," she recalled.

Lyndon Johnson returned to Washington, but the couple kept in touch with letters and phone calls. Just seven weeks later, on November 17, 1934, Johnson turned his proposal into a lifelong commitment. He traveled to Texas and insisted that Lady Bird marry him that very day. Flustered, but also in love, she

Lady Bird considered becoming either a teacher or a reporter after college. "But all that never happened," she once said, "because I met Lyndon."

Lyndon Johnson and Lady Bird Taylor were married in San Antonio, Texas. This photo is from their honeymoon in Mexico.

When Lyndon and Lady Bird got married in San Antonio, he forgot to bring a wedding ring. He sent a friend to a nearby department store to buy a temporary one. It cost $2.50.

After being reelected to the House of Representatives in 1940, Johnson celebrated his victory from a hospital bed. He was recovering from an **appendicitis** operation.

agreed. The ceremony hastily took place at a church in San Antonio. After the honeymoon, Lady Bird moved with Johnson to Washington.

But Kleberg soon fired Johnson. Some people said that Kleberg feared that Johnson was after his job. Johnson wasn't unemployed for long, however. Friends recommended him for the National Youth Administration (NYA). The NYA was one of the many programs that President Franklin Roosevelt had begun to help jobless Americans during the **Great Depression.** The Johnsons moved back home to Texas, where Lyndon would act as director of the state's NYA program.

Johnson was successful at his new job. Word spread that he was a man of action. In 1937, Johnson heard there was an opening in the U.S. Congress. He decided the time was right to run for office. He ran as a member of the Democratic Party, one of the two most powerful **political parties** in the country.

The election was tough. Eight other **candidates** from his area were running. Johnson searched for a way to stand out from the crowd. He claimed that he was the only candidate who truly supported President Roosevelt and his work. Roosevelt was a very popular president. Johnson's idea won him a seat in the House of Representatives. He was just 28 years old.

In 1940, Johnson ran for reelection. He won, but he soon realized that it would be years before he had enough **seniority** to make important decisions. In April of the following year, he saw an opportunity to move

ahead. Morris Sheppard, a U.S. senator from Texas, had died. His seat in the Senate was open. Johnson decided to run for the position. This meant he had to campaign all across the big state of Texas.

To reach voters, Johnson used radio ads. He was doing well until the governor of Texas, W. Lee "Pappy" O'Daniel, entered the race. O'Daniel was well known and popular. Still, Johnson was ahead the night of the election, and he even celebrated his victory. But when the votes were counted the next day, he learned that O'Daniel had won. Johnson and his supporters thought that O'Daniel's people might have cheated, but they could not prove it.

Johnson (right) shakes hands with President Franklin Roosevelt in 1937. Johnson strongly supported Roosevelt's policies.

Johnson didn't have time to feel sorry for himself. World War II was already raging in Europe and Asia. On December 7, 1941, the Japanese bombed Pearl Harbor in Hawaii. The United States entered the war the next day. Johnson, still a member of the House, was the first congressman who volunteered to serve. He became a lieutenant commander in the U.S. Navy. After a heroic air battle with the Japanese, Johnson was awarded the Silver Star, the third highest medal of valor in the armed forces.

One year later, President Roosevelt called all congressmen in the military back to the United States. It was time for them to return to work. Johnson's experiences in the war helped shape the ideas he held many years later when he was president and the nation

Johnson (second from right) reported for duty in the U.S. Navy on December 9, 1941—two days after the bombing of Pearl Harbor.

was struggling with the Vietnam War. "I learned that war comes about by two things," he said, "by a lust for power on the part of a few evil leaders and by a weakness on the part of the people whose love for peace too often displays a lack of courage that serves as an open invitation to all the aggressors of the world."

Lyndon Johnson in 1953

As Johnson returned to his work in Congress, he began to save money and make **investments,** such as buying property. The poverty of his youth had always haunted him. He wanted a secure life for himself and for his family. Lynda Bird, the Johnsons' first child, was born in 1944. Their second daughter, Luci Baines, arrived in 1947.

In 1948, Johnson again ran for the U.S. Senate, and this time he won. As a young senator, he was frustrated that he had so little power. But he worked hard, made friends with important senators, and was appointed to powerful committees. His power grew quickly and in 1953, Johnson became the Senate minority leader. The minority leader is the person who serves as the leader in the Senate for the party with fewer members in the Senate. He was the youngest senator to ever hold such an important position.

When Johnson was a senator, he and Lady Bird were invited to the White House for a reception. Afterward, Lady Bird wrote in her diary, "Tonight I went to my first (will it be my last and only!?!) dinner at the White House."

In 1954, Johnson was reelected to the Senate. After the election of 1954, there were more Democrats than Republicans in the Senate. Johnson became the majority leader. At last Johnson had the power he desired, but his work was very stressful. In 1955, it took a toll on his health. He suffered a major heart attack and spent four months recovering. He rested at the LBJ Ranch, a piece of land outside of Austin, Texas, which he had bought in the late 1940s.

After his health improved, Johnson returned to work. He helped pass the **Civil Rights** Act of 1957, which tried to protect the right of African Americans to vote. He also led a committee to advance space exploration. The committee passed the Space Act of 1958, which created the National Aeronautics and Space Administration (NASA).

Lyndon and Lady Bird Johnson sit with their daughters Luci (left) and Lynda in 1948.

JOHNSON STYLE

Lyndon Johnson was known for his powerful style of leadership. Many people called him an "operator" because he knew how to get things done—and done his way. Johnson had learned to get what he wanted by talking to the right people and saying the right things.

As president, Johnson wanted to pass his bills in Congress. He found out which members of Congress were against certain bills and why. Johnson then met with them to talk them into voting for his programs. He would flatter them and bully them. He used threats and humor. He would do whatever was needed to get their votes.

Although he was successful at working with Congress, Johnson sometimes ignored his staff and other people who helped him. The newspapers often talked about President Johnson's powerful style of leadership. They compared him to a king who ordered others to do as he commanded. Johnson didn't mind this talk. Such remarks did upset those who worked with the president, however. They wanted credit for helping him pass his programs through Congress and for helping him succeed.

CHAPTER THREE

INTO THE WHITE HOUSE

By 1960, Lyndon Johnson was recognized as a national leader of the Democratic Party. For several years, he had toyed with the idea of running for president, but he still wasn't sure. As others announced they would run, he held back. Some thought it was because Johnson had health problems. Others thought he wanted his fellow Democrats to usher him in with a huge show of support. Either way, he stalled until three days before the Democratic National **Convention** to announce he was a candidate.

All the time Johnson was considering running for president, John F. Kennedy was working hard to gain the **nomination.** At the convention, members of the party had to choose their candidate. They elected John F. Kennedy instead.

Lyndon Johnson was 55 years old when he became president.

Many party members still believed in Lyndon Johnson, however. They began to talk about choosing Johnson as the vice-presidential candidate. They thought Kennedy and Johnson would make a winning pair. Lady Bird Johnson approved of this idea. She was concerned about her husband's health. She believed that the job of vice president would be less stressful than her husband's position in the Senate. When John Kennedy asked Johnson to run with him, he gladly accepted. American voters liked Kennedy and Johnson. Kennedy won the presidency, and in January 1961, Johnson was sworn in as vice president of the United States.

John F. Kennedy (right), the Democratic candidate for president in 1960, was from Massachusetts. He chose Johnson as his vice-presidential candidate because he thought the Texan might help him win southern states.

Johnson supported the American space program. As vice president, he served as the chairman of the National Aeronautics and Space Council. He reported to President Kennedy that people could land on the moon as early as 1966 or 1967. It wasn't quite that soon, however. On July 16, 1969, Johnson attended the launch of *Apollo 11* at Florida's Cape Kennedy. Finally, on July 20, Johnson and the whole world watched as astronaut Neil Armstrong became the first person to walk on the moon.

Johnson played an active role as vice president. Like most vice presidents, he traveled to spread the word about the president's plans and programs. But Johnson traveled even more than most. He visited 34 countries. Johnson also served as chairman on two important committees, the President's Committee on Equal Employment Opportunity and the National Aeronautics and Space Council.

By 1963, the popular Kennedy-Johnson team began campaigning for the election of 1964. Then, on November 22, they made a fateful stop in Dallas, Texas. The president and first lady were riding in an open convertible car. Johnson was riding just two cars behind. Suddenly, a man named Lee Harvey Oswald shot and killed President Kennedy.

Johnson was stunned by Kennedy's **assassination,** and the United States was shaken. Johnson realized that the American people needed a strong voice to help them feel safe and calm. Just hours after Kennedy's death, Johnson took the oath of office as president of the United States. He soon talked to the current **cabinet** members and urged them to stay with him to finish the work President Kennedy had planned. Five days after Kennedy's murder, President Johnson addressed the nation on television. He vowed to carry on with Kennedy's programs.

The first issue President Johnson tackled was a tax cut, which would lower the taxes Americans had to pay. Some senators argued that this didn't make sense because the government needed all the money it earned

Lyndon Johnson was sworn in as president on Air Force One, *the presidential jet, on November 22, 1963. Jacqueline Kennedy (right), President Kennedy's widow, looked on.*

from taxes. Johnson looked at the nation's **budget** and cut spending from every department. In fact, he cut $500 million dollars from the budget. Congress finally agreed there was enough money for his tax cut.

One of Johnson's most important goals as president was to ensure civil rights for all Americans. Kennedy and Johnson shared a goal of ending **discrimination** against African Americans and other minorities in the country. President Johnson pleaded with the country to put their differences aside in memory of President Kennedy. "Let us put an end to the teaching and preaching of hate and evil and violence," he said.

The Lyndon B. Johnson Space Center near Houston, Texas, is named after Johnson in honor of his work with the space program.

Lyndon Johnson talks with civil rights leader Martin Luther King Jr. in the White House. President Johnson signed the Civil Rights Act of 1964, which banned segregation in public places.

Johnson pushed through the Civil Rights Act of 1964. Segregation laws had long kept African Americans from entering certain public places that were reserved for whites only, such as restrooms, hotels, and restaurants. The Civil Rights Act made such laws illegal. But even with this act, discrimination continued. African Americans still struggled for equal rights.

Another difficult issue that President Johnson faced was the war in Vietnam. The United States became involved in the war long before he became president. During President Harry Truman's term, the United

States had given money to France, which was the ruler of Vietnam at the time. Rebels led by a man named Ho Chi Minh began to fight against the French. They wanted Vietnam to be an independent nation. During the rebellion, Vietnam divided into two countries: North Vietnam, which was a **communist** country, and South Vietnam, which was not. The two sides were soon fighting each other.

Both President Dwight Eisenhower and President John Kennedy had sent money to help South Vietnam. President Kennedy had also sent 17,000 military advisers. They hoped to stop the spread of communism around the world. Johnson continued sending money, but he did not send any troops—at first.

During the 1964 presidential campaign, there were reports that the North Vietnamese had bombed an American destroyer in the Gulf of Tonkin. Although these reports were likely wrong, Johnson asked Congress to pass the Gulf of Tonkin Resolution. This act would allow him to take military action in Vietnam without actually declaring war. Looking back, many people believe that this action moved the United States toward a full war in Vietnam.

President Johnson chose Hubert Humphrey, a senator from Minnesota, as his vice presidential candidate. He felt confident during the campaign. Johnson told the people that the United States had "the opportunity to move not only toward the rich society and powerful society, but upward to the Great Society." The Republican Party chose Senator Barry Goldwater as its

Johnson loved dogs. He owned two beagles named Him and Her. After Him died in 1966, J. Edgar Hoover, the director of the Federal Bureau of Investigation, gave Johnson another beagle. The president named him J. Edgar.

Lady Bird Johnson wanted to make the world more attractive. She planted flower gardens at the White House and talked others into planting gardens around Washington.

candidate. Goldwater talked of using **nuclear weapons** on communist countries such as the **Soviet Union** and Vietnam. These powerful weapons could cause terrible destruction. Goldwater frightened many Americans.

Just before the election, President and Mrs. Johnson went to Texas to await the results. "It seems to me tonight that I have spent my whole life getting ready for this moment," Johnson said. When the votes were counted, he had won the election by a **landslide.** His supporters were rich and poor, from all walks of life and every race.

President Johnson set up the Texas White House, a large house on the LBJ Ranch outside of Austin, Texas. For years, Johnson took care of business from the Texas White House and often invited the nation's leaders there. They gathered outside on lawn chairs under the sprawling oak trees. Johnson felt comfortable at his second home and enjoyed working there.

Johnson loved spending time at his ranch in Texas. He's seen here rounding up cattle.

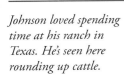

LADY BIRD'S LEGACY

As first lady, Lady Bird Johnson worked to advance her husband's dream but also supported her own causes. One dream they shared was to preserve nature. After Lyndon Johnson left office, Lady Bird began a project to promote the planting of wildflowers along the highways of Texas. She particularly supported the use of native plants. Starting in 1969, she gave awards to the highway districts that used native Texas plants as landscaping. The program at first amused some people. But today, the beauty of the wildflowers along Texas highways awe many drivers.

On her 70th birthday in 1982, Lady Bird celebrated the opening of the National Wildflower Research Center. Its purpose was to promote the use and preservation of native plants and wildflowers. The center grew into a hub for research and education about native plants and wildlife. The former first lady opened a new center in 1995 in Austin, which was named the Lady Bird Johnson Wildflower Center. It covers nearly 280 acres and houses more than 700 different kinds of plants. Lady Bird Johnson died on July 11, 2007, at age 94.

A TRYING END

Lyndon Johnson began his first elected term as president dedicated to his idea of the Great Society. He imagined a strong, successful country for all people no matter their color, age, or path through life. "The Great Society rests on abundance and liberty for all," he said. "It demands an end to poverty and racial injustice."

The first bill President Johnson signed was for a program called Medicare. The number of elderly people in the United States had doubled in the previous 20 years. The Medicare program gave people over age 65 health care that they could afford. Johnson followed this new law with one to increase funds for schools. He remembered his own experiences teaching poor children in Texas. He realized that education had helped him get all the way to the White

Lyndon Johnson went home to Texas after leaving the presidency.

House. President Kennedy had tried to pass a similar bill for a year without success. Johnson used his political skills to get it passed in just 87 days.

Despite his efforts to ensure civil rights for African Americans, racial problems continued to worsen. In the South, whites threatened blacks when they tried to vote. Police officers often stopped blacks from voting. In 1965, in Selma, Alabama, civil rights leader Martin Luther King Jr. led a drive to sign up three million black voters. The local sheriff, Jim Clark, arrested many of the organizers. Police officers clubbed or beat others.

*In 1965, **protesters** marched from Selma, Alabama, to Montgomery, Alabama. They marched to demand that the government protect African Americans' right to vote. The march took five days.*

Lyndon Johnson was the first president to appoint an African American to the U.S. Supreme Court. On June 13, 1967, Johnson named Thurgood Marshall, a civil rights leader, to sit on the highest court in the land.

To learn what others thought of him, Johnson installed three television sets in his office. This way, he could watch three stations at once. He also read the latest news from all across the country. To make sure his White House staff was loyal to him, Johnson even tape-recorded their conversations.

King and the other civil rights leaders did not back down. They organized a march of black and white people from Selma to the state capital of Montgomery. Sheriff Clark ordered the protesters to stop, but they did not. Clark and his men rode into the crowd and severely beat many people. They fired tear gas into the crowd to break up the group. This gas causes people's eyes to tear up so much that they cannot see.

King planned another march for two weeks later. President Johnson was unsure what to do. He wanted to protect the marchers with government troops. Yet Alabama governor George Wallace did not want him to send in troops. If he sent in troops against Wallace's wishes, Wallace would become a hero to other whites who were **prejudiced** against blacks. Johnson met with Wallace. He convinced Wallace that protecting the marchers was in his best interest. Wallace finally agreed to ask for troops, and the protestors held their march in peace.

The civil rights struggle inspired Johnson to create the most important act of his time in office: the Voting Rights Act. This act allowed the national government to supervise elections, ensuring that all Americans would be able to vote. Johnson asked Congress to pass the bill by arguing that the freedom promised in the U.S. **Constitution** was for every American citizen. Congress passed the bill in 1965.

Although Johnson had success with his Great Society program, he faced serious problems with Vietnam. By the mid-1960s, it looked as if South

*President Johnson
sometimes watched three
televisions at once.*

Vietnam would lose the war. In February 1965, the enemy attacked a U.S. airstrip in South Vietnam, killing eight Americans. President Johnson ordered U.S. forces to bomb the North Vietnamese. He continued the bombing for weeks. A month later, Johnson began to send ground troops to Vietnam.

Soon thousands of young men were sent to help the South Vietnamese fight against the communists. Congress still never formally declared that the United States was at war.

Sending U.S. troops to Vietnam did not work. It only resulted in more deaths on both sides. But Johnson felt he had to continue. He worried that if he didn't, the war might turn into World War III. Although most

Americans agreed with him at first, many grew tired of the senseless waste of human life. People began to protest U.S. involvement in the war even as President Johnson devoted more time to winning it.

As the 1968 election grew near, Johnson studied his chances for reelection. Senator Eugene McCarthy had entered as a Democrat with an antiwar message. President Kennedy's brother, Senator Robert Kennedy, also joined the contest. Johnson felt he still might win, but he needed to focus on the war, not on the election. His past health problems also worried him.

On March 31, Johnson addressed the nation on television. He said, "I shall not seek, and will not accept, the nomination of my party for another term as your president." He added that he would greatly reduce the bombing of North Vietnam in an effort to end the war.

Several days after Johnson's announcement, North Vietnamese leaders said they were willing to begin peace talks. The news relieved Johnson, but bad news quickly followed. Martin Luther King Jr. had been assassinated. As the shocked public reacted, Johnson used the event to further advance the civil rights cause. He passed a bill that had been stalled for two years—the Civil Rights Act of 1968. This act banned homeowners from discriminating against buyers because of their race. The bill passed just three days after Martin Luther King's funeral.

On October 31, the United States and North Vietnam began peace talks. Nothing came of the talks, however. Republican Richard Nixon became president in 1969. During his time in office, the war grew more intense. It would continue for five more years.

Johnson dropped out of public life after Nixon became president. He spent his retirement with Lady Bird, his daughters, and his grandchildren. He worked on writing his memoirs (the story of his life) and founded the LBJ Library and Museum in Austin.

Johnson suffered chest pains in 1970 and a second heart attack in 1972. Early the next year, President Nixon announced a cease-fire with North Vietnam. As the United States prepared to withdraw from the war, Lyndon Baines Johnson died on January 22, 1973, from a heart attack. He was buried on the LBJ Ranch next to the graves of his mother and father.

More than 56,000 American soldiers died in the Vietnam War.

Lady Bird Johnson often tried to get her husband to diet, but he refused. One night she was awakened by a clicking noise. She traced it to the kitchen and found Johnson eating one of his favorite desserts (tapioca pudding) with a metal spoon. The next day, Johnson asked for a wooden spoon so he wouldn't be caught in the future.

JOHNSON AND THE VIETNAM WAR

The Vietnam War was the most difficult issue of President Johnson's presidency. Even though he had great success on civil rights issues, many people only recall his problems with the war. By 1966, Johnson had sent nearly 400,000 American soldiers into battle. His Great Society programs came second to winning the war. In the picture below, President Johnson is greeting troops in Vietnam in 1966.

By 1967, President Johnson believed that the United States was close to a victory. He also believed that the American people would stand behind him. Many Americans grew angry that the war was dragging on. Antiwar protests broke out in cities across the country. People did not want to see Americans die for a war that had little to do with the United States. Protesters often chanted, "Hey, hey, LBJ! How many kids did you kill today?" In the picture to the right, protesters are marching in Washington, D.C., in 1967.

By 1967, more than half of Americans were against President Johnson's Vietnam policies. Still, Johnson told Americans that the war was going well. He told them that the North Vietnamese were a small force that would soon lose. But on January 31, 1968, the North Vietnamese and rebel groups in the south surprised the United States with a huge attack called the Tet offensive. It took place during the Tet holidays that celebrate the Vietnamese New Year.

Two thousand Americans died in the Tet offensive. U.S. citizens realized that North Vietnamese forces were not weak and small. They felt President Johnson had misled them. His popularity dropped. Johnson announced that he would not seek a second term in 1968. He said he needed to focus on winning the war instead of a campaign. The Vietnam War finally ended in 1973, the same year that Lyndon Johnson died.

T I M E   L I N E

1908
Lyndon Baines Johnson is born on August 27 on a farm outside of Stonewall, Texas.

1913
The Johnson family moves to nearby Johnson City.

1924
At age 15, Lyndon graduates from Johnson City High School.

1927
Lyndon enrolls in Southwest Texas State Teachers College in San Marcos, Texas.

1930
Johnson graduates from college with a degree in education.

1931
Congressman Richard Kleberg asks Johnson to move to Washington to work as his secretary.

1934
Johnson meets and falls in love with Claudia Alta (Lady Bird) Taylor. On November 17, they marry in San Antonio, Texas.

1935
Johnson is named the Texas director of President Franklin Roosevelt's National Youth Administration.

1937
Johnson is elected to the U.S. House of Representatives.

1940
Johnson is reelected to the House of Representatives.

1941
Johnson loses an election for the U.S. Senate. The Japanese bomb Pearl Harbor on December 7. Johnson, still a member of the House of Representatives, becomes the first member of Congress to volunteer for active duty in the armed forces.

1942
Johnson receives the Silver Star for bravery in action during an air combat mission. President Franklin Roosevelt orders all members of Congress in the armed forces to return to their offices.

1948
In November, Johnson wins election to the U.S. Senate.

1953
On January 2, Johnson is voted minority leader of the Senate.

1954
On November 2, Johnson is reelected to the Senate.

1955
Johnson is elected majority leader of the Senate. He is the youngest man ever to hold this position. He suffers his first heart attack and spends four months recovering.

1957
Johnson helps the Senate pass the Civil Rights Act of 1957.

1958
Johnson leads the Senate committee that helps establish the National Aeronautics and Space Administration (NASA).

1960
Johnson is elected vice president of the United States on November 8.

1961
Johnson is named chairman of the National Aeronautics and Space Council.

1963
On November 22, President Kennedy is assassinated in Dallas, Texas. Lyndon Johnson becomes the 36th president of the United States.

1964
Johnson signs the Civil Rights Act of 1964. Congress passes the Gulf of Tonkin Resolution. Johnson is nominated as the Democratic presidential candidate. On November 3, he is elected president of the United States. Hubert Humphrey is elected vice president.

1965
President Johnson takes the oath of office on January 20. He begins sending additional troops to Vietnam in the spring. On July 30, he signs the Medicare bill. On August 6, he signs the Voting Rights Act, which he later cites as the most important accomplishment of his presidency.

1968
Johnson announces that he will not be a candidate for another term as president, saying he wants to devote his time to ending the war, not to the election. Martin Luther King Jr. is assassinated in April. The Civil Rights Act is passed. The United States and North Vietnam begin peace talks in October.

1969
On January 20, Johnson returns to Texas and the LBJ Ranch after Richard M. Nixon is sworn in as president.

1971
On May 22, Johnson attends the dedication of the Lyndon Baines Johnson Library and Museum on the campus of the University of Texas at Austin.

1973
Lyndon Johnson dies at his ranch on January 22. He is buried in the family cemetery at the LBJ Ranch near his birthplace. U.S. participation in the Vietnam War ends.

1995
The Lady Bird Johnson Wildflower Center opens.

2007
On July 11, Lady Bird Johnson dies at the age of 94.

GLOSSARY

appendicitis (uh-pen-duh-SYE-tis)
Appendicitis is the swelling of the appendix, a tube in the lower torso. Johnson had an appendicitis operation in 1940.

assassination (uh-sass-ih-NAY-shun)
An assassination is a murder, especially of someone well-known. Johnson became president after the assassination of President John Kennedy.

budget (BUH-jit) A budget is a plan of how money will be used. Johnson looked at the nation's budget and cut spending from every department.

cabinet (KAB-nit) The cabinet is a president's group of advisers. After President Kennedy was assassinated, Johnson urged his cabinet to continue with his programs.

campaign (kam-PAYN) A campaign is the process of running for an election, including activities such as giving speeches or attending rallies. Welly K. Hopkins asked Johnson to help with his campaign.

candidates (KAN-duh-dayts) Candidates are people running in an election. Nine candidates were running for the open seat in Congress in 1937.

civil rights (SIH-vul RYTZ) Civil rights are the rights guaranteed by the Constitution to all citizens of the United States. Johnson helped pass the Civil Rights Act of 1957.

communist (KOM-yoo-nist) In a communist country, the government owns all businesses and controls the economy. North Vietnam was a communist country.

constitution (kon-stih-TOO-shun) A constitution is the set of basic principles that govern a state, country, or society. The U.S. Constitution promises certain rights to American citizens.

convention (kun-VEN-shun) A convention is a meeting. Political parties hold national conventions every four years to choose their presidential candidates.

debates (di-BAYTZ) Debates are competitions in which people discuss a question or topic, considering reasons for and against it. Johnson held debates between his students when he was a teacher.

discrimination (dis-krim-uh-NAY-shun)
Discrimination is the unfair treatment of people on the basis of race, religion, sex, or some other quality. Johnson tried to carry on President Kennedy's goal of ending discrimination.

Great Depression (GRAYT dee-PRESH-un)
The Great Depression was a period in U.S. history when there was little business activity, and many people could not find work. President Franklin Roosevelt started the National Youth Administration to help jobless people during the Great Depression.

investments (in-VEST-munts) Investments are amounts of money spent to make more money. During his time in Congress, Johnson began to make investments.

landslide (LAND-slyd) If a candidate wins an election by a landslide, he or she wins by a huge number of votes. Lyndon Johnson won the 1964 presidential election in a landslide.

legislature (LEH-jus-lay-chur) A legislature is the part of the government that makes laws. Lyndon Johnson's father served in the Texas state legislature.

native (NAY-tiv) Native refers to plants or animals that naturally live in a particular area. Lady Bird Johnson encouraged the use of native plants.

nomination (nom-ih-NAY-shun) If someone receives a nomination, he or she is chosen by a political party to run for office. Johnson did not seek the Democratic presidential nomination in 1968.

nuclear weapons (NOO-klee-ur WEH-punz) Nuclear weapons are weapons that produce hot, powerful explosions that can destroy an entire city. Senator Barry Goldwater suggested using nuclear weapons on communist countries.

political parties (puh-LIT-uh-kul PAR-teez) Political parties are groups of people who share similar ideas about how to run a government. Johnson was a member of the Democratic political party.

politics (PAWL-uh-tiks) Politics refers to the actions and practices of the government. Samuel Johnson was a farmer but wanted to work in politics.

prejudiced (PREJ-uh-dist) If people are prejudiced, they have a bad opinion about someone without good reason. Johnson did not want to make Governor Wallace a hero to white people who were prejudiced against African Americans.

protesters (PROH-test-urz) Protesters are people who hold marches to make their beliefs known. Martin Luther King Jr. led protesters in marches against discrimination.

segregation (seh-gruh-GAY-shun) Segregation is the practice of keeping black and white people apart. The Civil Rights Act of 1964 banned segregation laws.

seniority (seen-YOR-ih-tee) If people have seniority, they have held a position longer than other people. In Congress, members with seniority have the most power.

Soviet Union (SOH-vee-et YOON-yen) The Soviet Union was a large communist country in eastern Europe and central Asia. In 1991, it broke apart into Russia and several smaller countries.

THE UNITED STATES GOVERNMENT

The United States government is divided into three equal branches: the executive, the legislative, and the judicial. This division helps prevent abuses of power because each branch has to answer to the other two. No one branch can become too powerful.

EXECUTIVE BRANCH

PRESIDENT
VICE PRESIDENT
DEPARTMENTS

The job of the executive branch is to enforce the laws. It is headed by the president, who serves as the spokesperson for the United States around the world. The president signs bills into law and appoints important officials such as federal judges. He or she is also the commander in chief of the U.S. military. The president is assisted by the vice president, who takes over if the president dies or cannot carry out the duties of the office.

The executive branch also includes various departments, each focused on a specific topic. They include the Defense Department, the Justice Department, and the Agriculture Department. The department heads, along with other officials such as the vice president, serve as the president's closest advisers, called the cabinet.

LEGISLATIVE BRANCH

CONGRESS
Senate and
House of Representatives

The job of the legislative branch is to make the laws. It consists of Congress, which is divided into two parts: the Senate and the House of Representatives. The Senate has 100 members, and the House of Representatives has 435 members. Each state has two senators. The number of representatives a state has varies depending on the state's population.

Besides making laws, Congress also passes budgets and enacts taxes. In addition, it is responsible for declaring war, maintaining the military, and regulating trade with other countries.

JUDICIAL BRANCH

SUPREME COURT
COURTS OF APPEALS
DISTRICT COURTS

The job of the judicial branch is to interpret the laws. It consists of the nation's federal courts. Trials are held in district courts. During trials, judges must decide what laws mean and how they apply. Courts of appeals review the decisions made in district courts.

The nation's highest court is the Supreme Court. If someone disagrees with a court of appeals ruling, he or she can ask the Supreme Court to review it. The Supreme Court may refuse. The Supreme Court makes sure that decisions and laws do not violate the Constitution.

CHOOSING
THE PRESIDENT

It may seem odd, but American voters don't elect the president directly. Instead, the president is chosen using what is called the Electoral College.

Each state gets as many votes in the Electoral College as its combined total of senators and representatives in Congress. For example, Iowa has two senators and five representatives, so it gets seven electoral votes. Although the District of Columbia does not have any voting members in Congress, it gets three electoral votes. Usually, the candidate who wins the most votes in any given state receives all of that state's electoral votes.

To become president, a candidate must get more than half of the Electoral College votes. There are a total of 538 votes in the Electoral College, so a candidate needs 270 votes to win. If nobody receives 270 Electoral College votes, the House of Representatives chooses the president.

With the Electoral College system, the person who receives the most votes nationwide does not always receive the most electoral votes. This happened most recently in 2000, when Al Gore received half a million more national votes than George W. Bush. Bush became president because he had more Electoral College votes.

THE WHITE HOUSE

The White House is the official home of the president of the United States. It is located at 1600 Pennsylvania Avenue NW in Washington, D.C. In 1792, a contest was held to select the architect who would design the president's home. James Hoban won. Construction took eight years.

The first president, George Washington, never lived in the White House. The second president, John Adams, moved into the house in 1800, though the inside was not yet complete. During the War of 1812, British soldiers burned down much of the White House. It was rebuilt several years later.

The White House was changed through the years. Porches were added, and President Theodore Roosevelt added the West Wing. President William Taft changed the shape of the presidential office, making it into the famous Oval Office. While Harry Truman was president, the old house was discovered to be structurally weak. All the walls were reinforced with steel, and the rooms were rebuilt.

Today, the White House has 132 rooms (including 35 bathrooms), 28 fireplaces, and 3 elevators. It takes 570 gallons of paint to cover the outside of the six-story building. The White House provides the president with many ways to relax. It includes a putting green, a jogging track, a swimming pool, a tennis court, and beautifully landscaped gardens. The White House also has a movie theater, a billiard room, and a one-lane bowling alley.

PRESIDENTIAL PERKS

The job of president of the United States is challenging. It is probably one of the most stressful jobs in the world. Because of this, presidents are paid well, though not nearly as well as the leaders of large corporations. In 2007, the president earned $400,000 a year. Presidents also receive extra benefits that make the demanding job a little more appealing.

★ **Camp David:** In the 1940s, President Franklin D. Roosevelt chose this heavily wooded spot in the mountains of Maryland to be the presidential retreat, where presidents can relax. Even though it is a retreat, world business is conducted there. Most famously, President Jimmy Carter met with Middle Eastern leaders at Camp David in 1978. The result was a peace agreement between Israel and Egypt.

★ *Air Force One*: The president flies on a jet called *Air Force One*. It is a Boeing 747-200B that has been modified to meet the president's needs.

Air Force One is the size of a large home. It is equipped with a dining room, sleeping quarters, a conference room, and office space. It also has two kitchens that can provide food for up to 50 people.

★ **The Secret Service:** While not the most glamorous of the president's perks, the Secret Service is one of the most important. The Secret Service is a group of highly trained agents who protect the president and the president's family.

★ **The Presidential State Car:** The presidential limousine is a stretch Cadillac DTS.

It has been armored to protect the president in case of attack. Inside the plush car are a foldaway desk, an entertainment center, and a communications console.

★ **The Food:** The White House has five chefs who will make any food the president wants. The White House also has an extensive wine collection.

★ **Retirement:** A former president receives a pension, or retirement pay, of just under $180,000 a year. Former presidents also receive Secret Service protection for the rest of their lives.

F A C T S

QUALIFICATIONS

To run for president, a candidate must

* be at least 35 years old
* be a citizen who was born in the United States
* have lived in the United States for 14 years

TERM OF OFFICE

A president's term of office is four years.
No president can stay in office for more than two terms.

ELECTION DATE

The presidential election takes place every four years on the first Tuesday of November.

INAUGURATION DATE

Presidents are inaugurated on January 20.

OATH OF OFFICE

I do solemnly swear I will faithfully execute the office of the President of the United States and will to the best of my ability preserve, protect, and defend the Constitution of the United States.

WRITE A LETTER TO THE PRESIDENT

One of the best things about being a U.S. citizen is that Americans get to participate in their government. They can speak out if they feel government leaders aren't doing their jobs. They can also praise leaders who are going the extra mile. Do you have something you'd like the president to do? Should the president worry more about the environment and encourage people to recycle? Should the government spend more money on our schools? You can write a letter to the president to say how you feel!

1600 Pennsylvania Avenue
Washington, D.C. 20500
You can even send an e-mail to: president@whitehouse.gov

BOOKS

Appelt, Kathi. *Miss Lady Bird's Wildflowers: How a First Lady Changed America*. New York: Harper Collins, 2005.

Bausum, Ann. *Freedom Riders: John Lewis and Jim Zwerg on the Front Lines of the Civil Rights Movement*. Des Moines, IA: National Geographic, 2005.

Casad, Mary Brooke. *Bluebonnet at Johnson Space Center*. Gretna, LA: Pelican Publishing Company, 2003.

Medina, Loreta M. *The Turbulent 60s*. San Diego: Greenhaven Press, 2004.

Sommer, Shelley. *John F. Kennedy: His Life and Legacy*. New York: Harper Collins, 2005.

Venezia, Mike. *Lyndon B. Johnson: Thirty-Sixth President 1963–1969*. New York: Children's Press, 2007.

Vietnam War. New York: DK Eyewitness Books, 2005.

VIDEOS

The History Channel Presents The Presidents. DVD (New York: A&E Home Video, 2005).

National Geographic's Inside the White House. DVD (Washington, DC: National Geographic Video, 2003).

INTERNET SITES

Visit our Web page for lots of links about Lyndon Baines Johnson and other U.S. presidents:

http://www.childsworld.com/links

Note to Parents, Teachers, and Librarians: We routinely verify our Web links to make sure they are safe, active sites—so encourage your readers to check them out!

INDEX